PRIDE AND PREJUDICE

AN AQA ESSAY WRITING GUIDE

FABIENNE MARSHALL

SERIES EDITOR: R. P. DAVIS

First published in 2021 by Accolade Tuition Ltd
71-75 Shelton Street
Covent Garden
London WC2H 9JQ
www.accoladetuition.com
info@accoladetuition.com

With thanks to Miranda Matthews for her proofreading expertise.

ISBN 978-1-913988-04-3

FIRST EDITION
1 3 5 7 9 10 8 6 4 2

CONTENTS

FOREWORD

In your GCSE English Literature exam, you will be presented with an extract from Jane Austen's *Pride and Prejudice* and a question that asks you to offer both a close analysis of the extract plus a commentary of the novella as a whole. Of course, there are many methods one *might* use to tackle this style of question. However, there is one particular technique which, due to its sophistication, most readily allows students to unlock the highest marks: namely, **the thematic method**.

To be clear, this study guide is *not* intended to walk you through the novel scene-by-scene: there are many great guides out there that do just that. No, this guide, by sifting through a series of mock exam questions, will demonstrate *how* to organise a response thematically and thus write a stellar essay: a skill we believe no other study guide adequately covers!

I have encountered students who have structured their essays all sorts of ways: some by writing about the extract line by line, others by identifying various language techniques and giving each its own paragraph. The method I'm advocating, on the other hand, involves picking out three to four themes that will allow you to holistically answer the question: these three to four themes will become the three to four content paragraphs of your essay, cushioned between a brief introduction and conclusion. Ideally, these themes will follow from one to the next to create a flowing argument. Within each of these thematic paragraphs, you can then ensure you are jumping through the mark scheme's hoops.

So to break things down further, each thematic paragraph will include various point-scoring components. In each paragraph, you will quote from the extract, offer analyses of these quotes, then discuss how the specific language techniques you have identified illustrate the theme you're discussing. In each paragraph, you will also discuss how other parts of the novel further illustrate the theme (or even complicate it). And in each, you will comment on the era in which the novel was written and how that helps to understand the chosen theme.

Don't worry if this all feels daunting. Throughout this guide, Fabienne (the author!) will be illustrating in great detail – by means of examples – how to build an essay of this kind.

The Austenian equivalent of a selfie.

The beauty of the thematic approach is that, once you have your themes, you suddenly have a direction and a trajectory, and this makes essay writing a whole lot easier. However, it must also be noted that extracting themes in the first place is something students often find tricky. I have come across many candidates who understand the extract and the novel inside out; but when they are presented with a question under exam conditions, and the pressure kicks in, they find it tough to break their response down into themes. The fact of the matter is: the process is a *creative* one and the best themes require a bit of imagination.

In this guide, Fabienne shall take seven different exam-style questions, coupled with extracts from the novel, and put together a plan for each – a plan that illustrates in detail how we will be satisfying the mark scheme's criteria. Please do keep in mind that, when operating under timed conditions, your plans will necessarily be less detailed than those that appear in this volume.

Now, you might be asking whether three or four themes is best. The truth is, you should do whatever you feel most comfortable with: the examiner is looking for an original, creative answer, and not sitting there counting the themes. So if you think you are quick enough to cover four, then great. However, if you would rather do three to make sure you do each theme justice, that's also fine. I sometimes suggest that my student pick four themes, but make the fourth one smaller – sort of like an afterthought, or an observation that turns things on their head. That way, if they feel they won't have time to explore this fourth theme in its own right, they can always give it a quick mention in the conclusion instead.

Since 2017, Jane Austen has appeared on £10 notes issued
by the Bank of England.

Before I hand you over to Fabienne, I believe it to be worth-
while to run through the four Assessment Objectives the exam
board want you to cover in your response – if only to demonstrate how effective the thematic response can be. I would
argue that the first Assessment Objective (AO1) – the one that
wants candidates to 'read, understand and respond to texts' and
which is worth 12 of the total 34 marks up for grabs – will be
wholly satisfied by selecting strong themes, then fleshing them
out with quotes. Indeed, when it comes to identifying the top-
scoring candidates for AO1, the mark scheme explicitly tells
examiners to look for a 'critical, exploratory, conceptualised
response' that makes 'judicious use of precise references' – the
word 'concept' is a synonym of theme, and 'judicious references' simply refers to quotes that appropriately support the
theme you've chosen.

The second Assessment Objective (AO2) – which is also responsible for 12 marks – asks students to 'analyse the language, form and structure used by a writer to create meanings and effects, using relevant subject terminology where appropriate.' As noted, you will already be quoting from the novella as you back up your themes, and it is a natural progression to then analyse the language techniques used. In fact, this is far more effective than simply observing language techniques (personification here, alliteration there), because by discussing how the language techniques relate to and shape the theme, you will also be demonstrating how the writer 'create[s] meanings and effects.'

Now, in my experience, language analysis is the most important element of AO2 – perhaps 8 of the 12 marks will go towards language analysis. You will also notice, however, that AO2 asks students to comment on 'form and structure.' Again, the thematic approach has your back – because though simply jamming in a point on form or structure will feel jarring, when you bring these points up while discussing a theme, as a means to further a thematic argument, you will again organically be discussing the way it 'create[s] meanings and effects.'

AO3 requires you to 'show understanding of the relationships between texts and the contexts in which they were written' and is responsible for a more modest 6 marks in total. These are easy enough to weave into a thematic; indeed, the theme gives the student a chance to bring up context in a relevant and fitting way. After all, you don't want it to look like you've just shoehorned a contextual factoid into the mix.

Finally, you have AO4 – known also as "spelling and grammar." There are four marks up for grabs here. Truth be told, this guide is not geared towards AO4. My advice? Make sure

you are reading plenty of books and articles, because the more
you read, the better your spelling and grammar will be. Also,
before the exam, perhaps make a list of words you struggle to
spell but often find yourself using in essays, and commit them
to memory.

My (and Fabienne's) hope is that this book, by demonstrating
how to tease out themes from an extract, will help you feel
more confident in doing so yourself. I believe it is also worth
mentioning that the themes that have picked out in the course
of this guide are by no means definitive. Asked the very same
question, someone else may pick out different themes, and
write an answer that is just as good (if not better!). Obviously,
the exam is not likely to be fun – my memory of them is pretty
much the exact opposite. But still, this is one of the very few
chances that you will get at GCSE level to actually be creative.
And to my mind at least, that was always more enjoyable – if
enjoyable is the right word – than simply demonstrating that I
had memorised loads of facts.

In this extract, the Bennet family meet Mr Bingley and Mr Darcy for the first time, at an assembly in Meryton.

Mr Bingley was good looking and gentlemanlike; he had a pleasant countenance, and easy, unaffected manners. His sisters were fine women, with an air of decided fashion. His brother-in-law, Mr Hurst, merely looked the gentleman; but his friend Mr Darcy soon drew the attention of the room by his fine, tall person, handsome features, noble mien; and the report which was in general circulation within five minutes after his entrance, of his having ten thousand a year. The gentlemen pronounced him to be a fine figure of a man, the ladies declared he was much handsomer than Mr Bingley, and he was looked at with great admiration for about half the evening, till his manners gave a disgust which turned the tide of his popularity; for he was discovered to be proud, to be above his company, and above being pleased; and not all his large estate in Derbyshire could then save him from having a most forbidding, disagreeable countenance, and being unworthy to be compared with his friend.

Mr Bingley had soon made himself acquainted with all the principal people in the room; he was lively and unreserved, danced every dance, was angry that the ball closed so early, and talked of giving one himself at Netherfield. Such amiable qualities must speak for themselves. What a contrast between him and his friend! Mr Darcy danced only once with Mrs Hurst and once with Miss Bingley, declined being introduced to any other lady, and spent the rest of the evening in walking about the room, speaking occasionally to one of his own party. His character was decided. He was the proudest, most disagreeable man in the world, and everybody hoped that he would never come there again. Amongst the most violent against him was Mrs Bennet, whose dislike of his general behaviour was sharpened into particular resentment by his having slighted one of her daughters.

Starting with this extract, explore how Austen depicts polite society's biases in *Pride and Prejudice*.

Write about:

• how Austen depicts polite society's biases in this extract.

• how Austen depicts polite society's biases in the novel as a whole.

Introduction

You want to keep the introduction fairly short and sweet, but also ensure it packs a punch – after all, you only have one chance to make a first impression on the examiner. I recommend starting the introduction with a short comment on historical context to score early AO3 marks. I would then suggest that you very quickly summarize the thematic gist of your essay.

In this instance, I score early AO3 marks by invoking a titbit of history that places *Pride and Prejudice* in context. After this, I keep things relatively brief, hinting at the approach I am about to take.

"Given Austen's preoccupation with society's foibles and mores, it is little surprise that Georgian England's changing social contours – particularly the rise of 'polite society' – frequently came under her gaze, and this is especially true in *Pride and Prejudice*.[1] Austen in this extract introduces Mr Darcy, a character initially construed as elitist and grand due to his noble social standing. However, as Austen describes Darcy's reception in Meryton, she conveys not only society's mercuriality, but also its bias in favour of good breeding and manners – as opposed to deeper, more profound qualities – as a means of calculating social worth."[2]

Theme/Paragraph One: Austen depicts the society at Meryton as fetishizing nobility; however, its distaste for Mr Darcy's haughtiness also reveals

how polite society ultimately prizes good manners and breeding above nobility.

- Austen's narrator, who can arguably be considered here as the disembodied voice of polite society, deploys a triple syntactical sentence structure when introducing Darcy in this extract's opening paragraph: the narrator talks of his 'tall person, handsome features, noble mien.' Collectively, these descriptors convey Darcy's attractiveness to the assembly. The final adjective, 'noble', hints at the reason for this allure, and draws attention to the fact that Darcy belongs to a higher social stratum than the assembly at large, since he has inherited wealth and land (the physical manifestation of which is his estate, Pemberley), and has ties to noble families, such as that of Lady Catherine de Bourgh. That his 'mien' is described as noble points to how his face shows the inherent quality of his nobility. [*AO2 for the close analysis of the language and for discussing how form shapes meaning*].

- However, Austen also demonstrates how society expects nobility to be accompanied by good breeding, as shown through the assembly's abrupt change of heart towards Mr Darcy: he goes from being of 'noble mien' to distastefully 'above his company.' This points to the importance of manners in conferring social status in the eyes of Georgian polite society. [*AO1 for advancing the argument with a judiciously selected quote; AO2 for the close analysis of the language*].

- In contrast to Darcy's antagonism to polite society (by Chapter 6 he is still derisively asserting that 'every savage can dance'), Mr Bingley demonstrates a deep attunement to the codes of conduct Meryton society expects him to manifest: he 'Was lively and unreserved, danced every dance, was angry that the ball closed so early, and talked of giving one himself at Netherfield'. As a result, although elsewhere in the novel it is made unequivocally clear that he is *not* from nobility – his family wealth, the reader is informed, is 'acquired by trade' – his manners ('such amiable qualities,' as the narrator puts it) still win him an admiration from Meryton society that elevates him above Darcy. [*AO1 for advancing the argument with a judiciously selected quote*].

Theme/Paragraph Two: Austen conveys, and gently lampoons, the bias Meryton's landed gentry exhibit in favour of those with deep pockets – indeed, the tacit goal of the older women present appears to be a financially advantageous marriage for each of their daughters.

- In this extract, Austen highlights the intrusive tendency of married wives in this social stratum to pry into the financial affairs of others: the narrator talks of 'the report which was in general circulation within five minutes after his entrance, of his having ten thousand a year'. The noun 'report' captures society's officiousness in discerning the wealth of an individual and harks back to Austen's description of Mrs Bennet in Chapter 1, whose 'business' was the marriage of her daughters to eligible bachelors. [*AO1 for advancing the argument with a judiciously selected quote; AO2 for the close analysis of the language*].

- The mercenary bias of polite society is satirically alluded to in the sentence proceeding the 'report' of Darcy's wealth, which contains an alliterative description of Darcy as a 'fine figure.' The subtle implication here is that Darcy's wealth has heightened his physical attractiveness in the eyes of this assembly – whereas Bingley, who only brings in five thousand a year by comparison, is necessarily perceived as less physically appealing. [*AO1 for advancing the argument with a judiciously selected quote; AO2 for the close analysis of the language*].

- Elsewhere in the novel: One might note that by equating financial concerns with marriage in the novel's very first line – 'It is a truth universally acknowledged, that a single man in possession of a good fortune, must be in want of a wife' – Austen mockingly hints at the landed gentry's obsession with wealth from the start, thereby placing structural emphasis on the theme. This obsession is perhaps best exemplified by Mrs Bennet – a character whose voice sometimes seems to reflect polite society's attitudes writ large, and who, despite disliking Mr Darcy, worships his wealth: 'What jewels, what carriages you shall have', she says delightedly to Elizabeth at the novel's close. [*AO1 for advancing the argument with a judiciously selected quote; AO2 for discussing how structure shapes meaning*].

Theme/Paragraph Three: Austen highlights polite society's bias towards superficial and reductive thinking – flaws that are placed in stark relief when pitted against the intelligence and compara-

tive self-awareness of characters such as Elizabeth.

- Austen uses superlatives to emphasise polite society's tendency to form superficial and changeable judgements, and its inability to understand the subtleties of human nature. In this extract, Mr Darcy is cast as the 'proudest, most disagreeable man' after declining to dance with the ladies present at the assembly – the use of hyperbolic superlatives suggesting that it is chiefly emotion, as opposed to rationality, driving the change in opinion.[3] The exaggeration continues in the next sentence, as the narrator observes how 'everybody hoped that he would never come there again' – the attendees wishing to punish Darcy with a banishment that is comically disproportionate to his perceived transgression.[4] However, polite society is depicted not just as oblivious to subtleties in people's character, but also cruelly fickle. Darcy's fall in standing, after all, is absurdly swift – so much so that it is likened to the turning of the tide ('the tide of [Darcy's] popularity' is said to turn). [*AO1 for advancing the argument with a judiciously selected quote; AO2 for the close analysis of the language*].
- Although Mrs Bennet might be occasionally considered as an embodiment of polite society's mores, her unwillingness to budge on her low opinion of Darcy throughout the novel – an opinion built on superficial first impressions – speaks volumes as to her character's particular stubbornness, as opposed to the more changeable opinions of society in general.
- *Elsewhere in the novel*: That polite society is too

reductive and heavy-handed with its character assessments is made all the more apparent when pitted against Elizabeth's more considered and nuanced approach. Whereas Mrs Bennett judges Mr Darcy reductively, and remains wedded to her first impression throughout the novel, until she finally approves of him as a husband for her daughter because of his wealth and estate, Elizabeth exhibits an open-mindedness that allows her assessment of Mr Darcy to eventually evolve. The sagacity of her approach is demonstrated when, in the novel's second volume, Elizabeth witnesses Darcy's impeccable manners towards her aunt and uncle, as well as his servants, at Pemberley, and comes to understand that what she had construed as haughtiness had in fact been, in part, social awkwardness.

Conclusion

I have covered all the themes I was hoping to in the paragraphs above. As a result, I will first make reference to a second (yet very much relevant) nineteenth century novel in a bid to mop up any remaining AO3 marks going spare. Then, in a final AO1-scoring flourish, I will wrap things up with a brief parting comment that revisits one of the essay's central argument.

"Austen's *Pride and Prejudice* contains highly satirical depictions of polite society's biases: the novel makes a show of their obsessions with wealth and manners, and their penchant for superficial, judgemental thinking; and given that these traits seem alive and well some thirty-five years later – Charlotte Bronte's eponymous protagonist in *Jane Eyre* (1847) attempts to navigate a similar polite-society minefield at Rochester's Thornfield Hall – it would appear that Austen's observations are astute. Yet perhaps most striking is how Austen deploys polite society's foibles and biases as a backdrop to Elizabeth's own development, as she goes from aligning with broader societal attitudes to becoming increasingly self-critical of her preconceptions and prejudices."

An illustration from H. M. Brock, depicting
the sequence in Chapter Six that sees Sir
William Lucas attempt to orchestrate a
dance between Mr Darcy and Elizabeth.

At this point in the novel Elizabeth visits Netherfield when Jane is ill, and she spends an evening with Mr Darcy and the Bingley family.

"Your list of the common extent of accomplishments," said Darcy, "has too much truth. The word is applied to many a woman who deserves it no otherwise than by netting a purse or covering a screen. But I am very far from agreeing with you in your estimation of ladies in general. I cannot boast of knowing more than half-a-dozen, in the whole range of my acquaintance, that are really accomplished."

"Nor I, I am sure," said Miss Bingley.

"Then," observed Elizabeth, "you must comprehend a great deal in your idea of an accomplished woman."

"Yes, I do comprehend a great deal in it."

"Oh! certainly," cried his faithful assistant, "no one can be really esteemed accomplished who does not greatly surpass what is usually met with. A woman must have a thorough knowledge of music, singing, drawing, dancing, and the modern languages, to deserve the word; and besides all this, she must possess a certain something in her air and manner of walking, the tone of her voice, her address and expressions, or the word will be but half-deserved."

"All this she must possess," added Darcy, "and to all this she must yet add something more substantial, in the improvement of her mind by extensive reading."

"I am no longer surprised at your knowing *only* six accomplished women. I rather wonder now at your knowing *any*."

"Are you so severe upon your own sex as to doubt the possibility of all this?"

"*I* never saw such a woman. *I* never saw such capacity, and taste, and application, and elegance, as you describe united."

Mrs. Hurst and Miss Bingley both cried out against the injustice of her implied doubt, and were both protesting that they knew many women who answered this description, when Mr. Hurst called them to order, with bitter complaints of their inattention to what was going forward. As all conversation was thereby at an end, Elizabeth soon afterwards left the room.

"Eliza Bennet," said Miss Bingley, when the door was closed on her, "is one of those young ladies who seek to recommend themselves to the other sex, by undervaluing their own; and with many men, I dare say, it succeeds. But, in my opinion, it is a paltry device, a very mean art."

Starting with this extract, explore how Austen presents Elizabeth Bennet as an independent-minded woman in *Pride and Prejudice*.

Write about:

• how Austen presents Elizabeth Bennet as independent-minded in this extract.

• how Austen presents Elizabeth Bennet as independent-minded in the novel as a whole.

Introduction

As I have suggested before, we want to start with an early AO3 point (this time, I am invoking a relevant late-eighteenth century text that helps place Austen's work in context). We then want to follow up with a quick nod to the themes we have in mind.

"Writing in the wake of Mary Wollstonecraft's seminal proto-feminist work, *The Vindication of the Rights of Women* (1792), it can be argued that Austen in many respects presents Elizabeth as a kind of Wollstonecraftian ideal: a woman unafraid to express an opinion; who places emphasis on rationality over false refinement, and rejects unrealistic patriarchal expectations.[1] In this extract, Austen demonstrates Elizabeth's independence of mind not only through her willingness to speak out and reject patriarchal expectations, but also by juxtaposing her to Caroline Bingley, an individual who takes care to adhere to these expectations." [2]

Theme/Paragraph One: Austen emphasises Elizabeth's independent-mindedness through her unabashed willingness to air her own opinions. These stand in stark contrast to the opinions of Miss Bingley, who merely parrots those of Mr Darcy.

- In this extract, Austen presents Elizabeth as being able to assert her own thoughts in conversation, rather than merely buttressing someone else's opinion. In response to Mr Darcy's and Miss Bingley's lengthy stipulations of what ought to constitute an accomplished woman, Elizabeth states that '*I* never saw such a woman, *I* never saw such capacity, and taste, and application, and elegance, as you describe, united.' The italicised and repeated use of 'I' centres Elizabeth's opinion and rebukes Darcy's assertions directly, the mere act of speaking out to challenge Darcy highlighting Elizabeth's independence of mind. [*AO1 for advancing the argument with a judiciously selected quote; AO2 for the close analysis of the language*].
- Elsewhere in the novel: One might note that Elizabeth speaks her mind to Darcy throughout the novel; and, as the narrator notes in the final chapter,

their dialogic sparring – and Elizabeth's 'lively, sportive manner' of addressing Mr Darcy – persists into their married life, too. Even in marriage, Elizabeth remains a Wollstonecraftian 'rational creature' who exercises her independence of mind at will. It could also be noted that when given the chance to form an eligible marriage with Mr Collins, Elizabeth refuses him, despite the incredulity of her friends and the anger of her mother. That it would have been a marriage approved by society is shown by Charlotte Lucas' swift acceptance of him in Elizabeth's place. This perhaps indicates Elizabeth's emotional independence more than any other of her actions, since in the family's financial position it would have been expected that Elizabeth would acquiesce, despite her own feelings. [*AO1 for advancing the argument with a judiciously selected quote*].

- Austen places Elizabeth's independence of mind in sharp contrast to that of Miss Bingley who, in her attempt to win Darcy's affections, obsequiously mirrors his opinions. After supporting Darcy's views in this extract, Miss Bingley is described as his 'faithful assistant'. The noun 'assistant' has mercantile, unromantic and detached connotations, whereas the adjective 'faithful' demonstrates Miss Bingley's obedience to his perspective: she does not have a distinct viewpoint in the way Elizabeth does. [*AO1 for advancing the argument with a judiciously selected quote; AO2 for the close analysis of the language*].

Theme/Paragraph Two: Elizabeth's independence is exemplified not only through the fact that she speaks her mind, but also in the substance of her opinion – she is pushing back on unrealistic expectations that have become almost a measure of a young woman's eligibility for marriage, but condemn most women to failure.

- Miss Bingley posits an absurd list of criteria for women to live up to – they ought to 'have a thorough knowledge of music, singing, drawing, dancing, and the modern languages,' she asserts – only to have Mr Darcy interject with another stipulation: they must further 'improve' their mind 'by extensive reading.' As a result, when Elizabeth responds with the assertion that 'she never saw such capacity, and taste, and application,' she is not merely asserting independence by daring to speak her mind, but also in her unwillingness to encourage unrealistic criteria that set women up for failure and disappointment. [*AO1 for advancing the argument with a judiciously selected quote; AO2 for the close analysis of the language*].

- Elsewhere in the novel: The idea that women's lives (of the middle or upper social classes) ought to revolve around cultivating a societally predetermined (and absurdly demanding) set of skills is pervasive in the novel. In Chapter 29, for instance, Lady Catherine de Bourgh, Mr Darcy's haughty and demanding aunt, expresses incredulity bordering on horror when Elizabeth reveals that she did not have a governess growing up, and was instead self-educated: 'No governess! How was that possible?' In a society where governesses were de rigueur for young women in the upper classes – the starting point on the path towards cultivating the skills listed by Miss Bingley and Mr Darcy – Elizabeth's exemption from a governess's influence perhaps gave rise to her atypical attitude in the first place. With all the force of the Bingley/Darcy opinions about womanhood against her, Elizabeth does not soften or retract her own argument, which again shows the strength of her independent mindset. [*AO1 for advancing the argument with a judiciously selected quote*].

- Towards the end of the extract, Miss Bingley contests that Elizabeth's mentality is in fact a form of flirtation: an attempt to 'recommend [herself] to the other sex by undervaluing [her] own.' That Miss Bingley is unable to conceive that Elizabeth may be arguing in good faith accentuates Elizabeth as an intellectual outlier. Just after this extract, Darcy's response to Miss Bingley: 'Undoubtedly...there is meanness in *all* the arts which ladies sometimes condescend to employ for captivation' might be taken to show that Darcy is aware of Miss Bingley's own 'arts' and that he is beginning to enjoy Elizabeth's unusual independence of mind despite himself. [*AO1 for advancing the argument with a judiciously selected quote; AO2 for the close analysis of the language*].

Theme/Paragraph Three: Beyond the demand that women cultivate an unrealistic skill-set, Elizabeth displays independence in her unwillingness to adopt the sort of refined comportment that

Miss Bingley considers essential in an accomplished woman.

- After enumerating the skills that women should aspire to cultivate, Miss Bingley in this extract also points to further stipulations for realising accomplished womanhood: the idea that a woman must have 'something in her air,' and, while elaborating, she points to 'the tone of her voice, her address and expressions.' This triple syntactical structure telegraphs an almost pedantic obsession with meeting these intangible criteria that encapsulate the concept of the ideal woman.[3] [*AO1 for advancing the argument with a judiciously selected quote; AO2 for the close analysis of the language and for discussing how form shapes meaning*].

- <u>Elsewhere in the novel</u>: Particularly telling, however, is the fact that Miss Bingley also notes that the accomplished woman must have a certain 'manner of walking.' This is no incidental detail. Prior to this extract, Elizabeth, after learning that her sister Jane is ill at Netherfield, walks three miles to tend to her – an act which elicits incredulity in Miss Bingley, who is shocked that Elizabeth would brave 'such dirty weather, and by herself,' and states that Elizabeth's hair is 'so untidy, so blowsy' – the disapproving repetition of 'so' buffeting Elizabeth as the wind had done. [*AO1 for advancing the argument with a judiciously selected quote; AO2 for the close analysis of the language*].

- Mere paragraphs prior to this extract (a proximity in the novel's structure that places emphasis on the motif – Miss Bingley explicitly criticises Elizabeth's manner of walking. Whereas for Miss Bingley the way one walks ought to be bent to the contemporary requirements of refined aesthetics, for Elizabeth walking – which she does frequently, over great distances – becomes another marker of her independence: literally, since it gives her mobility and agency; and symbolically, since it represents a deliberate rejection of refined codes of conduct. Earlier, Austen emphasised Elizabeth's individualism through her tendency to walk alone, by describing her as 'No horsewoman,' a real anomaly in the days when almost everybody rode. [*AO1 for advancing the argument with a judiciously selected quote; AO2 for discussing how structure shapes meaning; AO3 for acknowledging historical context*].

Conclusion

Although the essay above is meaty, I have one final observation about the extract – namely, the implication of Elizabeth exiting the room – and I have chosen to integrate it into the conclusion, so that the examiner is continuing to encounter fresh material right up until the end of my essay.

"Elizabeth in this extract finds herself rounded on by practically the entire party: not only Mr Darcy and Miss Bingley, but Mrs Hurst too 'crie[s] out against' Elizabeth's position. However, Austen emphasises Elizabeth's independence of mind not only through her refusal to back down, but through her actions: she literally goes away from the company: 'Elizabeth soon afterwards left the room'. This can be seen as a physical rebuff of her opponents' arguments. Yet Elizabeth's independence of mind is not only emphasised in the way she uses her body – be it by exiting the room, or walking – but also in how she deploys her voice to question the absurdities of patriarchal and societal expectations."

A banner commemorating Jane Austen. It was designed by the artist Mary Lowndes in 1908, and was displayed at a march in support of women's suffrage that same year.

This extract is found at the end of Elizabeth's visit to Netherfield to look after Jane during her illness. Mrs Bennet comes to see Jane and Elizabeth with her two youngest daughters.

Darcy only smiled; and the general pause which ensued made Elizabeth tremble lest her mother should be exposing herself again. She longed to speak but could think of nothing to say; and after a short silence Mrs. Bennet began repeating her thanks to Mr. Bingley for his kindness to Jane, with an apology for troubling him also with Lizzy. Mr. Bingley was unaffectedly civil in his answer, and forced his younger sister to be civil also, and say what the occasion required. She performed her part indeed without much graciousness, but Mrs. Bennet was satisfied, and soon afterwards ordered her carriage. Upon this signal, the youngest of her daughters put herself forward. The two girls had been whispering to each other during the whole visit, and the result of it was, that the youngest should tax Mr.

Bingley with having promised on his first coming into the country to give a ball at Netherfield.

Lydia was a stout, well-grown girl of fifteen, with a fine complexion and good-humoured countenance; a favourite with her mother, whose affection had brought her into public at an early age. She had high animal spirits, and a sort of natural self-consequence, which the attention of the officers, to whom her uncle's good dinners, and her own easy manners recommended her, had increased into assurance. She was very equal, therefore, to address Mr. Bingley on the subject of the ball, and abruptly reminded him of his promise; adding, that it would be the most shameful thing in the world if he did not keep it. His answer to this sudden attack was delightful to their mother's ear:

"I am perfectly ready, I assure you, to keep my engagement; and when your sister is recovered, you shall, if you please, name the very day of the ball. But you would not wish to be dancing while she is ill."

Lydia declared herself satisfied. "Oh! yes—it would be much better to wait till Jane was well, and by that time most likely Captain Carter would be at Meryton again. And when you have given *your* ball," she added, "I shall insist on their giving one also. I shall tell Colonel Forster it will be quite a shame if he does not."

Starting with this extract, explore how Austen presents Elizabeth's family members in *Pride and Prejudice*.

Write about:

• **how Austen presents Elizabeth's family members in this extract.**

• **how Austen presents Elizabeth's family members in the novel as a whole.**

Introduction

Historical context does not always need to be incredibly specific. That said, be careful to avoid being overly vague. For instance, merely asserting that women were treated as "weaker" in Austen's time is unlikely to impress. Instead, try to add more texture and sophistication.

"Considering that the social standing of women was in no small part determined by the lineage, dignity and good reputation of their family in the early nineteenth century, Elizabeth's family's comic excesses and indiscretions – which Austen explores in depth in this extract – have a direct and personal impact on Elizabeth. Whereas Elizabeth is acutely socially aware, her family are presented as agents of embarrassment with their scheming, social tone-deafness, and, in Lydia's case, sexual forwardness. It could be argued that in the different characters of the Bennet family, Austen has satirised most of the archetypes of contemporary folly."

Theme/Paragraph One: Austen presents Mrs Bennet as a would-be Machiavellian schemer, who

is intent on orchestrating financially expedient marriages for her daughters. [1]

- As Mrs Bennet is 'repeating' her thanks to Mr Bingley for 'his kindness' to Jane, the reader is invited to call to mind the fact that Jane came to be ill at Netherfield in the first place as a result of Mrs Bennet's scheme to try and match Jane romantically with Mr Bingley: Mrs Bennet is thanking him for his kindness, while secretly scheming to become his mother-in-law. Her apology for 'Troubling him with Lizzie' could arguably be a projection of her own feelings, since Elizabeth is the 'troubling' daughter in her mother's mind: an outlier who is not on board with her mother's machinations. [*AO1 for advancing the argument with a judiciously selected quote; AO2 for the close analysis of the language*].

- Elsewhere in the novel: Certainly, there is considerable irony when, in Chapter 7, just after learning that Jane had in fact fallen sick as a result of her mother's scheme for her to ride in the rain, Mrs Bennett exclaims that 'as long as she stays [at Netherfield], it is all very well,' since her daughter is of course in fact explicitly unwell. For Mrs Bennett, the success of her schemes takes precedence over her daughter's physical wellbeing, and Jane's sudden feverish illness could arguably be taken as Austen's metaphor for the unhealthiness of the scheme itself. [*AO1 for advancing the argument with a judiciously selected quote; AO2 for the close analysis of the language*].

- Yet Mrs Bennet is not alone in her scheming. Lydia too partakes in this behaviour, albeit with considerably less subtlety, as she attempts in this extract to coax Mr Bingley into holding a ball. That her ambushing of, or 'sudden attack' on Mr Bingley with her forward remarks is described as 'delightful in her mother's ear' suggests that Mrs Bennet sees and approves her own penchant for scheming reflected in Lydia's gambit. [*AO1 for advancing the argument with a judiciously selected quote*].

Theme/Paragraph Two: Austen could be using the presentation of the Bennets' lack of social awareness in this extract to show a key difference between Elizabeth and the rest of her family. The reader feels Elizabeth's humiliation at her mother's and sister's brash behaviour

- Although Mrs Bennet is a schemer – someone who attempts to pull social levers – she proves to be astonishingly oblivious to social nuance; indeed, Austen in this extract takes care to capture Elizabeth's acute embarrassment at her mother's social bluntness and lack of tact. That a pause in Mrs Bennet's and Mr Bingley's conversation 'made Elizabeth tremble lest her mother should be exposing herself again' is especially telling: not only does the word 'again' suggest Mrs Bennet has revealed her embarrassing deficiency in manners at least once already, but the phrase 'exposing herself' – words evocative of nakedness – point to the profundity of embarrassment induced. Further, the trochaic word 'tremble,' with its shuddering ictus on the first syllable, seems almost to mimic the trembling Elizabeth experiences, further emphasising the impact Mrs Bennet's obliviousness has on Elizabeth.[2] [*AO1 for advancing the argument with a judiciously selected quote; AO2 for the close analysis of the language and for discussing how form shapes meaning*].

- Whereas Mrs Bennet reveals her lack of social awareness through her indiscretions, Lydia on the other hand does so via her excessive forwardness. Towards the end of the extract, the fifteen-year-old Lydia tells Mr Bingley that it would be 'the most shameful thing in the world' if he were not to hold a ball. The use of the superlative: the '*most* shameful thing' demonstrates the tactlessly hyperbolic nature of Lydia's speech. Her spoken intention to '*tell*' Colonel Forster to also hold a ball arguably sounds like a boast, deliberately letting the people present know of her power over men in general. [*AO1 for advancing the argument with a judiciously selected quote; AO2 for the close analysis of the language*].

- Elsewhere in the novel: The lack of social awareness in the Bennet family is not confined to this extract: Elizabeth's family – with the exception of Jane – time and again betray their deficiencies in manners. Mr Bennet's imperious command to Mary to 'Let the other young ladies have time to exhibit' during the assembly in Chapter 18, for example, draws attention to Mary's lack of social graces, while also demonstrating Mr Bennet's disregard for how the implication that Mary is monopolising the limelight would humiliate her in such a public setting. [*AO1 for advancing the argument with a judiciously selected quote*].

- Yet, apart from his dislike of society and his awkward

social skills, Elizabeth's father is in some ways the family member to whom she is most similar, and he refuses to join his wife in persuading Elizabeth to marry Mr Collins, whom he and Elizabeth both make fun of with their lively wit. They share a sense of the ridiculous, and she is his favourite, as he reveals when he jokingly says that if Mr Bingley should want to marry one of his daughters, he 'must throw in a good word for my little Lizzie.' [*AO1 for advancing the argument with a judiciously selected quote*].

Theme/Paragraph Three: Whereas Austen presents Elizabeth as witty and independent, her younger sisters Lydia and Kitty are depicted as inappropriately flirtatious, overly impulsive and flippant.

- Beyond her scheming and tactlessness – both exemplified by her demand that Mr Bingley host a ball – Lydia is also characterized as excessively flirtatious and imprudent. The first hint is the reference to her 'high animal spirits,' a phrase that, while evocative of a certain innocence, also hints at a thoughtlessness and lack of rational discernment: she behaves with the lack of forethought that an excited animal might demonstrate. Her 'Oh!' when Bingley remarks that she would surely not want a ball while Jane was ill, tells the reader that she had no thought for her sister, but only for her own amusement. That this impulsiveness bleeds over into her interactions with men is alluded to both obliquely and explicitly. The fact that her 'easy' manner elicits 'attention from the officers' in the militia is telling, whereas her openly stated desire to wait till Captain Carter has returned to attend the ball: 'Captain Carter would be at Meryton again' more explicitly points to her capricious, uninhibited approach to the opposite sex. [*AO1 for advancing the argument with a judiciously selected quote; AO2 for the close analysis of the language*].

- Elsewhere in the novel: Lydia's unchecked reckless behaviour reaches its denouement with her elopement with a member of the very same militia alluded to in this extract: namely Mr Wickham. Austen reveals the depths of Lydia's fecklessness via Lydia's letter to Harriet Forster sent at the time of her elopement: a structural device that gives direct insight into Lydia's mindset. Particularly striking in the missive is the repeated mention of laughter – 'I cannot help laughing;' 'can hardly write for laughing' – which underlines the flippancy with which Lydia approaches serious proceedings: she eloped, seemingly, for the fun of it. [*AO1 for advancing the argument with a judiciously selected quote; AO2 for the close analysis of the language and for discussing how structure shapes meaning*].

- Austen appears to use the epistolary tradition to further emphasise Lydia's character flaws. Whereas letters in novels of the period were used to relay matters of emotional heft – be they the zealous musings of Robert Walton in Shelley's *Frankenstein*, or the love messages in Emily Bronte's *Wuthering Heights* – Austen again points to Lydia's superficiality of character by having her debase the means of communication with her glib tone. [*AO3 for placing the text in literary context*].

Conclusion

Since the extract encouraged us to pay more attention to some members of Elizabeth's family than others, I have opted to use the conclusion to somewhat counteract this, and ensure that all of the family members are given some "air time."

"In this extract we see the silliness of Lydia, the social vulgarity of Mrs Bennet and the good sense and discernment of Elizabeth. The kindness and sweet nature of Jane, the tiresome sanctimony of Mary and the easily influenced personality of Kitty, as well as the clever but ineffective character of Mr Bennet are shown clearly elsewhere in the novel and allow Austen to set her satirical eye on many diverse subjects within one family. The through-line as the novel unfolds is Austen's third person narrator, who at times satirises Elizabeth's family by aping their voices, and at others bluntly points out their foibles."

A t this point, almost a third of the way through the novel, Elizabeth takes the chance to have a private conversation with the charming Mr Wickham for the first time.

Elizabeth was again deep in thought, and after a time exclaimed, "To treat in such a manner the godson, the friend, the favourite of his father!" She could have added, "A young man, too, like *you*, whose very countenance may vouch for your being amiable"—but she contented herself with, "and one, too, who had probably been his own companion from childhood, connected together, as I think you said, in the closest manner!"

"We were born in the same parish, within the same park; the greatest part of our youth was passed together; inmates of the same house, sharing the same amusements, objects of the same parental care. *My* father began life in the profession which your uncle, Mr. Phillips, appears to do so much credit to—but he gave up every thing to be of use to the late Mr. Darcy and devoted all his time to the care of the Pemberley property. He was most highly esteemed by Mr. Darcy, a most intimate, confidential friend. Mr. Darcy often acknowledged himself to be under the greatest obligations to my father's active superintendence, and when, immediately before my father's death, Mr. Darcy gave him a voluntary promise of providing for me, I am convinced that he felt it to be as much a debt of gratitude to *him*, as of his affection to myself."

"How strange!" cried Elizabeth. "How abominable! I wonder that the very pride of this Mr. Darcy has not made him just to you! If from no better motive, that he should not have been too proud to be dishonest—for dishonesty I must call it."

"It *is* wonderful," replied Wickham, "for almost all his actions may be traced to pride; and pride has often been his best friend. It has connected him nearer with virtue than any other feeling. But we are none of us consistent; and in his behaviour to me, there were stronger impulses even than pride."

"Can such abominable pride as his, have ever done him good?"

"Yes. It has often led him to be liberal and generous, to give his money freely, to display hospitality, to assist his tenants, and relieve the poor. Family pride, and *filial* pride, for he is very proud of what his father was, have done this. Not to appear to disgrace his family, to degenerate from the popular qualities, or lose the influence of the Pemberley House, is a powerful motive. He has also *brotherly* pride, which, with *some* brotherly affection, makes him a very kind and careful guardian of his sister, and you will hear him generally cried up as the most attentive and best of brothers."

Starting with this extract, explore how Austen presents pride in *Pride and Prejudice.*

Write about:

• **how Austen presents the theme of pride in this extract.**

• **how Austen presents the theme of pride in this novel as a whole.**

Introduction

Invoking other nineteenth century novels in a relevant way – as I have done below – is a great tactic for picking up AO3 contextual marks.

"Be it the haughty Ingrams of Charlotte Bronte's *Jane Eyre* or Dickens's embittered Mrs Sparsit of the lapsed Powler family in *Hard Times*, individuals with a surfeit of pride appear time and again in nineteenth century fiction as objects of fascination. Although Mr Wickham, here in his first intimate conversation with Elizabeth, is an arch-dissembler, his assertions of pride's capacity to incite jealousy and other character flaws still hold water. Yet perhaps most interesting here is how Elizabeth's injured pride functions to cloud her judgement of Mr Wickham, and how her own erroneous belief in Darcy's arrogant pride encourages her to believe Wickham's lies."

Theme/Paragraph One: Austen presents pride as a damaging flaw as it cultivates superiority from a character's peers.

- Wickham in this extract deliberately crafts a false narrative in which Mr Darcy's pride has led to vindictiveness. Wickham first takes pains to subtly suggest that, in childhood, he and Mr Darcy were, in many respects, peers: the refrain of 'same' in 'born in the same parish, within the same park' is engineered to insinuate that, despite being born to separate families, they entered the world as social equals. Having once established this backdrop, Wickham presents Mr Darcy as jealous of the fact that Darcy's father had great affection for Wickham ('the favourite of his father' as Elizabeth alliteratively puts it), and exacted financial retribution. In Wickham's telling, Darcy's pride becomes a source of undue and unjust vindictiveness. [*AO1 for advancing the argument with a judiciously selected quote; AO2 for the close analysis of the language*].

- Elsewhere in the novel: While Wickham's story is of course a misrepresentation, in many ways pride *is* shown to lead to toxic character flaws in Austen's novel. Indeed, Darcy's comportment when he first appears at Meryton – which happens to be the first time the word 'proud' appears in the text, thereby structurally linking the trait to Darcy – does hint at an unpleasant sense of self-superiority; and although the assembly's view that he is 'above his company, and above being pleased' is later shown to be reductive and unfair, it still contains some vestige of truth. [*AO1 for advancing the argument with a judiciously selected quote; AO2 for the close analysis of the language and for discussing how structure shapes meaning*].

- It might also be contended that Wickham's own ignoble dissembling in this extract is itself partially borne of pride: a desire not to be exposed for his wrongdoings and to be considered as the wronged hero of the story by Elizabeth, further underlining the notion that pride spawns toxic behaviour.

Theme/Paragraph Two: Austen uses Wickham to broach the idea of familial pride. Although Wickham rightly suggests it to be a source of haughtiness and arrogance, he also unfairly attempts to imply it induces selfishness in Mr Darcy when dealing with those beyond his family.

- In this extract, Wickham goes to great lengths to paint Darcy as being intensely proud of his family, and, in particular, of his ancestry. When Wickham identifies 'filial pride' in Darcy, and notes that Darcy 'is very proud of what his father was,' he is pointing to the pride Darcy feels not only towards his father, but also, implicitly, towards his ancestry as a whole: after all, left unsaid is the idea that 'what his father was' depended on whom *his* father was in turn. Again, while Wickham is deliberately attempting to smear Darcy, there is nevertheless truth in the idea that Darcy draws a sense of superiority from his ancestral standing, and, in spite of not having a title, uses it to cast himself as a member of the nobility (as opposed to the mere landed gentry). [*AO1 for advancing the argument with a judiciously selected quote; AO2 for the close analysis of the language*].

- Indeed, Austen treats this sense of loftiness drawn from familial pedigree with a healthy dose of satire throughout the novel; with Lady Catherine de Bourgh's attempts to hark back to a grandiose family tree, and Mr Collins' exaggerated worship of her nobility being two important sources of humour in the novel.

- Wickham also attempts to use Darcy's excessive familial pride as a means of painting him as selfish. For one thing, he insinuates that any 'liberal and generous' behaviour exhibited by Darcy does not stem from genuine kindness, but out of a desire to 'not to appear to disgrace his family.' For another, by using hyperbolic terms to sing Darcy's praises regarding his treatment of his sister Georgiana Darcy (Wickham calls him a 'very careful guardian to his sister' and the 'most attentive' brother), Wickham hints that Darcy has in fact been given too much credit, and insinuates that his kindness towards his sister, borne of 'brotherly pride,' is to the exclusion of those outside his family. Yet while Darcy does prove to be proud of his lineage – perhaps even overly so – the events of the novel rebuff Wickham's insinuations. Not only does Darcy's later letter to Elizabeth show that Darcy had indeed gone above and beyond for his sister, but his subsequent efforts to aid Lydia suggest that familial pride does not stop him from helping others. [*AO1 for advancing the argument with a judiciously selected quote; AO2 for the close analysis of the language*].

Theme/Paragraph Three: Austen demonstrates how injured pride can also obscure even the most discerning characters from making accurate judgements.

- By placing a number of exclamatory remarks in Elizabeth's mouth, Austen hints that Elizabeth in this extract has to some degree been misled into forming an unfairly negative opinion of Mr Darcy. In reaction to Mr Wickham's account of how Mr Darcy ignored his late father's wishes of providing for Mr Wickham, Elizabeth's remarks – 'How strange!'; 'How abominable!' – drip with indignation and disbelief. Although Elizabeth's credulity is at least in part due to Wickham's duplicitous charm – he is described as exceedingly 'amiable' and personable – one must also note the part played by injured pride and its impact on Elizabeth's capacity for rational discernment. Because Mr Darcy refused to dance with her at that initial ball, Elizabeth's bruised pride leaves her susceptible to believing the worst of Mr Darcy. [*AO1 for advancing the argument with a judiciously selected quote; AO2 for the close analysis of the language*].

- One might note, however, that even as injured pride clouds Elizabeth's judgment in this instance, she still on some level seems to intuit the inconsistency of Wickham's story, expressing astonishment 'that the very pride of this Mr Darcy [had] not made him just to [Mr Wickham]!' Elizabeth also shows forbearance by stopping herself from too early an intimacy with Wickham: her first instincts are to compliment him on his appearance: 'a young man like *you*, whose very countenance may vouch for your being amiable', but, unlike her mother and her sister Lydia, she thinks before she speaks, and expresses herself in a less intimate manner. [*AO1 for advancing the argument with a judiciously selected quote; AO2 for the close analysis of the language*].

- Elsewhere in the novel: Indeed, although Elizabeth allows her injured pride to get the best of her in this instance, she later comes to realise how injured pride results in false impressions which makes an individual 'blind, partial, prejudiced, absurd.' In her epiphanic moment after Mr Darcy's letter concerning Mr Wickham, Elizabeth observes how she had 'gratified [her] vanity in useless or blameable mistrust!' – acknowledging how her injured vanity and pride led to fallacious judgements.[1] [*AO1 for advancing the argument with a judiciously selected quote; AO2 for the close analysis of the language*].

Conclusion

"At one point in the novel, Elizabeth's sister Mary proclaims that 'Pride...is a very common failing'. Austen uses irony here, since Mary herself has a misplaced pride in her own wisdom. Yet pride's universality is indeed one of the most striking qualities in this novel: it seems to touch each and every character. Considered as the very worst of the deadly sins in contemporary Christian teachings, it is not surprising that the study of pride in its many forms was of compelling interest to novelists of the time. However, though presented as a multifaceted phenomenon – one that inspires haughtiness and deceit, complicates relations to one's family, and, when injured, clouds judgement – it is ultimately presented as most impactful during first impressions, since individuals mediate their opinions of each other through their own sense of pride, and these opinions often then dictate the action that ensues. With this in mind, it is perhaps unsurprising that Austen's original title for the novel was *First Impressions*."

An illustration from H. M. Brock,
depicting Mr Wickham's first appearance
in Chapter Fifteen.

This passage, coming at the centre of the novel, describes Elizabeth's reaction to Darcy's letter explaining his actions concerning her sister Jane, Mr Bingley and Mr Wickham.

In this perturbed state of mind, with thoughts that could rest on nothing, she walked on; but it would not do; in half a minute the letter was unfolded again, and collecting herself as well as she could, she again began the mortifying perusal of all that related to Wickham, and commanded herself so far as to examine the meaning of every sentence. The account of his connection with the Pemberley family was exactly what he had related himself; and the kindness of the late Mr. Darcy, though she had not before known its extent, agreed equally well with his own words. So far, each recital confirmed the other; but when she came to the will, the difference was great. What Wickham had said of the living was fresh in her memory, and as she recalled his very words, it was impossible not to feel that there was gross duplicity on one side or the other; and, for a few moments, she flattered herself that her wishes did not err. But when she read and re-read with the closest attention, the particulars immediately following of Wickham's resigning all pretensions to the living, of his receiving in lieu so considerable a sum as three thousand pounds, again was she forced to hesitate. She put down the letter, weighed every circumstance with what she meant to be impartiality—deliberated on the probability of each statement—but with little success. On both sides it was only assertion. Again she read on; but every line proved more clearly that the affair, which she had believed it impossible that any contrivance could so represent, as to render Mr. Darcy's conduct in it less than infamous, was capable of a turn which must make him entirely blameless throughout the whole.

The extravagance and general profligacy which he scrupled not to lay at Mr. Wickham's charge, exceedingly shocked her; the more so, as she could bring no proof of its injustice. She had never heard of him before his entrance into the ——shire Militia, in which he had engaged at the persuasion of the young man who, on meeting him accidentally in town, had there renewed a slight acquaintance. Of his former way of life nothing had been known in Hertfordshire but what he told himself. As to his real character, had information been in her power, she had never felt a wish of inquiring. His countenance, voice, and manner had established him at once in the possession of every virtue.

Starting with this extract, explore how Austen presents the importance of solitary contemplation.

Write about:

• **how Austen presents the importance of solitary contemplation in this extract.**

• **how Austen presents the importance of solitary contemplation in the novel as a whole.**

Introduction

We can score AO3 marks not only by referring to other texts and the historical period in general, but also by discussing the novel's own publication history. The titbit below, which brings up the original title of Austen's work, is a good one to remember, since social interactions and first impressions are so integral to the novel.

"Given that the minefield of social interactions is so central to this novel – indeed, the original title of Austen's novel was *First Impressions*, a nod to how initial social encounters drive the action – it is perhaps unsurprising that solitary contemplation has an important role as a counterpoint to judgements made in the heat of the moment. Aside from offering a means to bring about personal growth, this extract – in which Elizabeth digests Darcy's letter regarding Mr Wickham – demonstrates how solitary contemplation offers a means of investigating the fallacious charms of others and questioning one's own prejudices."

Theme/Paragraph One: Austen highlights the importance of solitary contemplation by presenting it as a tough, intensive activity that takes strain to engage in, and thus, tacitly, as a means of working towards personal growth.

- As Elizabeth engages in contemplation in this passage – more specifically, the re-evaluation of Mr Darcy and Mr Wickham – what is perhaps most striking (once she has overcome her initial anger) is the sense of strain as she processes the new information. The reader is told her that she 'read and re-read with the closest attention,' the superlative 'closest' indicating the meticulousness and the repetition of 'read' ensuring that the reader is forced to digest the same word twice, further hammering home Elizabeth's intellectual process.[1] Moreover, the form itself indicates the depth of her thought: not only is the extract constructed of two large paragraphs, each reflecting continuous bodies of thought, but the sentence in which she is 'weigh[ing] every circumstance]' itself has an interpolated clause ('deliberated on the probability of each statement'), the strain on the syntax mirroring Elizabeth's strenuous mental athletics. [*AO1 for advancing the argument with a judiciously selected quote; AO2 for the close analysis of the language and for discussing how form and structure shapes meaning*].
- The strain becomes a way of telegraphing the fact that contemplation is a form of work. More specifically, by putting in the work of questioning her assumptions,

Austen seems to tacitly be suggesting that Elizabeth is working towards self-improvement – a process that distinguishes her from those individuals who lack the objectivity to question their first impressions.

- Elsewhere in the novel: Often Austen appears to demonstrate characters' strength though their ability to do the work of questioning their assumptions and amending their opinions. Mr Darcy, as well as Elizabeth, exhibits this trait. In a passage at the end of the novel, when Mr Darcy refers to the letter that formed the basis for this extract, Mr Darcy acknowledges that his 'behaviour [to Elizabeth] … was unpardonable.' Mr Darcy, through personal contemplation, has been able to rectify his previous biases. [*AO1 for advancing the argument with a judiciously selected quote*].

Theme/Paragraph Two: Austen could be said to demonstrate the virtues of solitary contemplation by showing how it is capable of counteracting prejudices and deceptive external influences. The characters in *Pride and Prejudice* who spend time in self-contemplation contrast strongly with those who are too shallow or too self-important to do so.

- One key influence Elizabeth is battling against in this extract is her prejudice against Darcy, which began with injured pride from their original meeting, when he refused to dance with her and made a slighting remark about her looks. However, Austen demonstrates how solitary contemplation allows Elizabeth to interrogate these prejudices. A key moment in this extract is when, through the free indirect discourse, the reader learns that while Elizabeth had assumed it impossible for Darcy to come across as nothing less than 'infamous,' the revelations in the letter suggests he may be 'entirely blameless on the whole.'[2] Elizabeth, through solitary contemplation, is able to directly acknowledge her prejudice – her determination to think the worst of Darcy – and confront it with honesty. [*AO1 for advancing the argument with a judiciously selected quote; AO2 for the close analysis of the language*].

- Elsewhere in the novel: The other key influence Elizabeth is seen to counteract with her contemplations in the extract is the malign dissembling of Mr Wickham. Mr Wickham's powers of persuasion are established early on, the narrator asserting in Chapter 16 that 'the commonest, dullest, most threadbare topic might be rendered interesting by [Wickham's] skill [as a] speaker' – the triple syntactical sentence structure, together with the almost serpentine sibilance ('skill...speaker') adding emphasis to his conversational prowess. It might be noted that Wickham shares many similarities with the charismatic Willoughby in Austen's *Sense and Sensibility,* who deludes impressionable Marianne and even, for a while, the sensible Elinor; indeed, both men might be considered reimaginings of the restoration character of the Rake, the charmer with ulterior and self-interested motivations. [*AO1 for advancing the argument with a judiciously selected quote; AO2 for the close analysis of the language*].

- Wickham's powers of persuasion are reaffirmed in this extract, as Elizabeth ponders how 'His countenance, voice, and manner had established him at once in the possession of every virtue.' However, on this occasion, Elizabeth, as she engages in solitary contemplation, begins to dig beneath Wickham's charming veneer, and for the first time begins to interrogate his background and reliability: 'Of his former way of life nothing had been known in Hertfordshire but what he told himself.' Wickham, along with Mrs Bennet, Lydia, Kitty, Mary, Mr Collins and Lady Catherine de Bourgh, are the characters who, whether for lack of sense or an excess of self-importance, cannot be imagined as having the ability to self-contemplate, and they are the characters in the novel whom Austen appears to satirise most enthusiastically. [*AO 1 for advancing the argument with a judiciously selected quote*].

Theme/Paragraph Three: Solitary contemplation functions as a narrative mechanism that allows the reader to decode and interpret information in tandem with the character, who, it can be argued, acts as a surrogate reader within the novel. [3]

- The chapter immediately prior to this extract features the explanatory letter from Darcy. In a sense, Elizabeth is cast as a surrogate reader embedded within the novel: her solitary contemplation, conveyed through the free indirect narrative, offers a rubric that guides the reader in how to decode and interpret the letter, while also allowing the reader to juxtapose their own interpretations with Elizabeth's. For instance, when Elizabeth reflects how 'each recital' –

that is, both Wickham's and Darcy's –'confirmed the other' on the history between Wickham and Darcy's father, 'but when she came to the will, the difference was great,' her solitary contemplation functions to not only refresh the reader's memory of Wickham's narrative and draw attention to the significance Elizabeth personally places on this detail, it also invites the reader to compare the details that caught their eye to those that caught Elizabeth's. [*AO1 for advancing the argument with a judiciously selected quote; AO2 for the close analysis of the language*].

- However, Elizabeth's solitary contemplations do not just offer a surrogate reading of this letter, but also offer a set of emotional responses that the reader is invited to take as vicarious prompts. When, for example, the reader is informed that Elizabeth 'began the mortifying perusal,' it is telegraphing to the reader that they too ought to be mortified. That she is 'exceedingly shocked' at Darcy's restraint in portraying Wickham is also an invitation to share in her own shock. [*AO1 for advancing the argument with a judiciously selected quote*]

Conclusion

"Although Austen's novel might have originally been titled *First Impressions*, it is striking that solitary contemplation proves just as central to the novel's mechanics as social dynamics. Aside from offering a path to personal growth and an antidote to the prejudices that arise from first impressions, solitary contemplation is also cast as a crucial mechanism to allow the reader to chart the inner workings of Elizabeth's mind. Elizabeth can arguably be cast as a kind of surrogate reader within the novel, helping the reader decode and understand events."

' She stood several minutes before the picture, in earnest contemplation.'

An illustration by C. E. Brock (brother to the previous Illustrator mentioned in this guide). It depicts Elizabeth contemplating a portrait in Chapter Forty-Three.

T his extract is found at a critical moment of the book where Lydia elopes with Mr Wickham under his pretence of getting married.

Jane then took it from her pocket-book, and gave it to Elizabeth. These were the contents:

"My dear Harriet,
"You will laugh when you know where I am gone, and I cannot help laughing myself at your surprise to-morrow morning, as soon as I am missed. I am going to Gretna Green, and if you cannot guess with who, I shall think you a simpleton, for there is but one man in the world I love, and he is an angel. I should never be happy without him, so think it no harm to be off. You need not send them word at Longbourn of my going, if you do not like it, for it will make the surprise the greater, when I write to

them and sign my name 'Lydia Wickham.' What a good joke it will be! I can hardly write for laughing. Pray make my excuses to Pratt for not keeping my engagement, and dancing with him to-night. Tell him I hope he will excuse me when he knows all; and tell him I will dance with him at the next ball we meet, with great pleasure. I shall send for my clothes when I get to Longbourn; but I wish you would tell Sally to mend a great slit in my worked muslin gown before they are packed up. Good-bye. Give my love to Colonel Forster. I hope you will drink to our good journey.

"Your affectionate friend,
"LYDIA BENNET."

"Oh! thoughtless, thoughtless Lydia!" cried Elizabeth when she had finished it. "What a letter is this, to be written at such a moment! But at least it shows that *she* was serious on the subject of their journey. Whatever he might afterwards persuade her to, it was not on her side a *scheme* of infamy. My poor father! how he must have felt it!"

"I never saw anyone so shocked. He could not speak a word for full ten minutes. My mother was taken ill immediately, and the whole house in such confusion!"

"Oh! Jane," cried Elizabeth, "was there a servant belonging to it who did not know the whole story before the end of the day?"

Starting with this extract, explore how Austen presents morality and reputation in *Pride and Prejudice*.

Write about:

• **how Austen presents morality and reputation in this extract.**

• **how Austen presents morality and reputation in the novel as a whole**

Introduction

"It is perhaps unsurprising that allusions to reputation and morality are recurrent through *Pride and Prejudice*: as the middle classes swelled, Georgian society became increasingly dependent on manners and morals to calculate status, as inherited wealth became less crucial in the calculus. This extract explores how, for young women, their perceived morality was inextricably bound to their sexual propriety, and how any transgression on this front would be cataclysmic not only for their own reputation, but for that of their family, too.[1] Austen also uses the character of Wickham to demonstrate how the veneer of a good reputation can enable morally repugnant behaviour."

Theme/Paragraph One: Austen explores how, for young women, their moral worth in the eyes of society – and thus their reputation – was pinned to their sexual propriety, though Lydia demonstrates a reckless disregard for this dynamic.

- Austen in this extract explores the damage Lydia does to her own moral standing by eloping with Wickham, in the process laying bare how nineteenth century society equated a woman's sexual purity with her all-important reputation. That Lydia is eloping in the first place is made clear through the reference to 'Gretna Green,' a small Scottish village that also doubled up as a contemporary euphemism for eloping against one's parents' wishes. The notion that this will strike a blow to Lydia's moral reputation is, however, most forcefully communicated through Elizabeth's reaction to the letter. By suggesting that Lydia had not adequately thought through her actions – 'Oh! thoughtless, thoughtless Lydia!' – Elizabeth implies there are compelling reasons for her *not* to have acted thus, and chief among them is the implication for her sexual, and thus moral, standing. Further, that Elizabeth frets about servants gossiping ('was there a servant ... who did not know... before the end of the day') not only reemphasises the salaciousness of the transgression, but also hints at how quickly a perceived moral transgression – particularly a sexual one – can destroy a reputation.[2] [*AO1 for advancing the argument with a judiciously selected quote; AO2 for the close analysis of the language*].
- However, as Elizabeth notes, Lydia herself is portrayed as blasé about the implications of this affair for her future 'good name'. Austen's structural choice to implant a letter here gives us access to Lydia's first-person narrative, and reveals Lydia to be nonchalant about elopement, hence her constant reference to laughter: she 'cannot help laughing'. [*AO2 for discussing how structure shapes meaning*].

- Elsewhere in the novel: Although Elizabeth does not seem to dispute the equation of sexual propriety with moral standing here, she does perceive more nuance than the societal view which seeks to frame Lydia's action as a death-knoll for her reputation, for Elizabeth notes that Lydia was not in fact the instigator: 'it was not on her side a *scheme* of infamy.' The dramatic, overwrought reaction of other characters suggests that Austen, too, felt that the hit to a young woman's reputation in response to such a transgression was disproportionate: Mr Collins's alliterative assertion that the 'death of your daughter would have been a blessing,' seeking as it does to yoke the oxymoronic words 'death' and 'blessing,' points to a deeply muddled moral code, and recalls Leonato's cry after his daughter Hero's disgrace in *Much Ado About Nothing*: 'Death is the fairest cover for her shame that may be wished for.' [*AO1 for advancing the argument with a judiciously selected quote; AO2 for the close analysis of the language; AO3 for invoking literary context*].

Theme/Paragraph Two: Austen shows how a blow to an individual's moral standing and reputation can have a devastating impact on the moral standing of that individual's family as a whole.

- It is striking here that not only does Elizabeth exhibit a very personal distress upon hearing news of Lydia's elopement, but she also articulates anxiety about her father's wellbeing: 'My poor father! How he must have felt it!' Certainly, the dual exclamation marks and staccato sentences seem to demonstrate how keenly Elizabeth empathises with her father's suffering.[3] Yet it is vital to appreciate that Mr Bennet's suffering here is not merely borne of sympathy for the self-inflicted damage Lydia has done to her own reputation. Rather, because a family's reputation was impacted by any single family member's indiscretion, Mr Bennet's suffering might come from his painful awareness of the consequences for himself, his wife and his other daughters. [*AO1 for advancing the argument with a judiciously selected quote; AO2 for the close analysis of the language and for discussing how form shapes meaning; AO3 for demonstrating an awareness of historical context*].

- Elsewhere in the novel: This dynamic is more explicitly spelt out in Elizabeth's later comments to her father, and her observation that 'Our importance, our respectability in the world must be affected by the wild volatility' Lydia exhibits, the repeated use of 'our' spelling out the collective nature of a family's responsibility. As Mr Collins succinctly puts it, Lydia's behaviour ends up 'injurious to the fortunes of all the others.' [*AO1 for advancing the argument with a judiciously selected quote; AO2 for the close analysis of the language*].

Theme/Paragraph Three: It could be argued that Austen depicts Mr Wickham as a case study of how the veneer of even a little-known but superficially good reputation can facilitate deception and immoral actions.

- In Lydia's letter, Lydia (obliviously) assigns Mr

Wickham a highly ironic sobriquet, referring to him 'an angel.' While the reader, along with Elizabeth and Jane, is able to perceive how misled Lydia has been at this point in the novel, it is worth noting that Wickham had earlier been successful at pulling the wool over the eyes of society at large, and had been considered 'amiable' at Meryton. Elizabeth at one time even briefly considered him as a possible suitor for herself, and talking with another officer at the Netherfield ball, was gratified to hear that Wickham was 'universally liked.' [*AO1 for advancing the argument with judiciously selected quotes*].

- However, as the novel unfolds, Austen provides greater insight into Mr Wickham's character, allowing the reader to see beyond his agreeable and talkative veneer to glimpse his true manipulative nature; to see a discrepancy between his original reputation in Meryton and his true distorted morals. When Elizabeth remarks to Jane on reading the letter that 'whatever he might afterwards persuade her to, it was not on her side a *scheme* of infamy', she is not only partially exonerating her sister, who clearly expected to be soon married, but also further indicting Wickham as a deliberate seducer.[4] The verb 'persuade' and the italicisation of 'scheme' further emphasises Wickham's ensnarement of Lydia, and his ruthless exploitation of her naive infatuation. This manipulative but charming character was a recurrent trope in nineteenth century novels: the character of the Rake sought to seduce women into eloping with them, often resulting in their social and physical ruin. Henry Crawford in Austen's *Mansfield Park* and John Willoughby in *Sense and Sensibility* are similar in their seductive charisma, suggesting perhaps that the writer found this type of character a particularly interesting study. [*AO1 for advancing the argument with a judiciously selected quote; AO2 for the close analysis of the language; AO3 for placing text in its literary and historical context*].

Conclusion

"Perhaps the most climactic scene in Charlotte Bronte's *Jane Eyre* sees the eponymous protagonist's wedding with Rochester thwarted after Jane's relative gets wind that Rochester had been concealing a pre-existing wife from Jane: the novel makes clear that had the marriage gone ahead under such circumstances, it would have devastated Jane's reputation. Austen's novel similarly presents the relationship between a woman's sexual conduct and her social reputation, but also examines in greater depth how a woman's reputation was tied to that of her entire family. Yet whereas Bronte's Rochester, though deceptive, is portrayed somewhat sympathetically, Wickham's exploitation of his good reputation is portrayed as far more unequivocally cruel."

This extract is found towards the end of the novel, when Elizabeth thanks Mr Darcy for assisting her sister Lydia in her marriage to the deceitful Mr Wickham.

"You must not blame my aunt. Lydia's thoughtlessness first betrayed to me that you had been concerned in the matter; and, of course, I could not rest till I knew the particulars. Let me thank you again and again, in the name of all my family, for that generous compassion which induced you to take so much trouble, and bear so many mortifications, for the sake of discovering them."

"If you *will* thank me," he replied, "let it be for yourself alone. That the wish of giving happiness to you might add force to the other inducements which led me on, I shall not attempt to deny. But your *family* owe me nothing. Much as I respect them, I believe I thought only of *you*."

Elizabeth was too much embarrassed to say a word. After a short pause, her companion added, "You are too generous to trifle with me. If your feelings are still what they were last April, tell me so at once. *My* affections and wishes are unchanged, but one word from you will silence me on this subject for ever."

Elizabeth, feeling all the more than common awkwardness and anxiety of his situation, now forced herself to speak; and immediately, though not very fluently, gave him to understand that her sentiments had undergone so material a change, since the period to which he alluded, as to make her receive with gratitude and pleasure his present assurances. The happiness which this reply produced, was such as he had probably never felt before; and he expressed himself on the occasion as sensibly and as warmly as a man violently in love can be supposed to do. Had Elizabeth been able to encounter his eye, she might have seen how well the expression of heartfelt delight, diffused over his face, became him; but, though she could not look, she could listen, and he told her of feelings, which, in proving of what importance she was to him, made his affection every moment more valuable.

They walked on, without knowing in what direction. There was too much to be thought, and felt, and said, for attention to any other objects. She soon learnt that they were indebted for their present good understanding to the efforts of his aunt, who *did* call on him in her return through London, and there relate her journey to Longbourn, its motive, and the substance of her conversation with Elizabeth; dwelling emphatically on every expression of the latter which, in her ladyship's apprehension, peculiarly denoted her perverseness and assurance; in the belief that such a relation must assist her endeavours to obtain that promise from her nephew which *she* had refused to give. But, unluckily for her ladyship, its effect had been exactly contrariwise.

Starting with this extract, explore how Austen presents love in *Pride and Prejudice*.

Write about:

• **how Austen presents love in this extract.**

• **how Austen presents love in the novel as a whole.**

Introduction

"The trials, tribulations and complexities of love were a recurring concern in the Regency Era novel, whether in Fanny Burney's *Cecilia*, or such seminal Jane Austen texts as *Sense and Sensibility* and *Emma*. Austen's *Pride and Prejudice* – with its central romance between Elizabeth and Mr Darcy, which has a stuttering start but gathers pace in the novel's final chapters – similarly places the topic under the microscope. However, Austen's exploration of Elizabeth and Darcy's relationship amongst the other 'love matches' within the novel not only allows the author to explore the ways love can manifest between two individuals, but also love's capacity to overcome social divides."

Theme/Paragraph One: By placing respectful, even deferential, language in Mr Darcy's mouth, Austen arguably portrays a form of substantive love, built on esteem and consideration.

- As Mr Darcy replies to Elizabeth's words of gratitude in this extract, his language is strikingly deferential: he observes that while he respects Elizabeth's family, his focus was on Elizabeth herself: 'Much as I respect them, I believe I thought only of *you*.' The word 'respect' here is particularly potent; indeed, given that the respect Mr Darcy articulates for Elizabeth's family appears to be trumped by his feelings towards Elizabeth, the suggestion is that his feelings towards Elizabeth in fact *surpass* mere 'respect.' [*AO1 for advancing the argument with a judiciously selected quote; AO2 for the close analysis of the language*].

- This sense that Mr Darcy's attitude towards Elizabeth goes beyond respect is underscored by the way he frames his marriage proposal in this extract: if a marriage proposal is implicitly an act of submission, the phraseology Darcy employs, which emphasises his absolute obedience to Elizabeth's decision – 'one word from you will silence me on this subject for ever' – places his deference at the core of his proposal. That this sensitive mode of speech stands in such stark contrast to Mr Darcy's first marriage proposal, in which he harshly explained how he could not overcome his affections for Elizabeth despite his pride in his superior familial connections, allows Austen to convey a belief that a substantive loving relationship is one built not on haughty expectations, but on respect and courtesy. Given that marriage law in the Regency

Era conceived of the wife as a 'feme covert' – originally a French term indicating that married women legally belonged to their husband – Austen's vision of a loving relationship predicated on mutual respect was strikingly progressive for her time. [*AO1 for advancing the argument with a judiciously selected quote; AO2 for the close analysis of the language; AO3 for placing the text in historical context*].

- Elsewhere in the novel: This proposal can be juxtaposed not only with Mr Darcy's earlier proposal, but also with that of Mr Collins, who, in response to Elizabeth's rebuff, haughtily contends that her 'refusal of [his] addresses is merely words of course.' Whereas Darcy requires simply a 'word' from Elizabeth to silence him – an indication of the significance he assigns to Elizabeth's words – Mr Collins views Elizabeth's words as just so much noise: 'merely words.' [*AO1 for advancing the argument with a judiciously selected quote; AO2 for the close analysis of the language*].

Theme/Paragraph Two: As Austen delves into the dynamic between Elizabeth and Mr Darcy, Austen not only presents a version of paradigmatic respectful love, but also explores how this strain of love can overwhelm those in such a relationship. [1]

- A key factor at play in this extract is the degree to which both Mr Darcy and Elizabeth find themselves overwhelmed by the love they experience for one another. Elizabeth is initially presented as lost for words as a result of feeling abashed; she was 'embarrassed to say a word'. She cannot even meet Darcy's eyes, and keeps her own cast down. Yet as this motif of hobbled articulation continues – she is struck by 'more than common awkwardness and anxiety' and, when she finally 'force[s] herself to speak' she does so 'not very fluently' – it becomes increasingly clear that embarrassment is not solely responsible. Rather, the implication is that her love for Darcy has overrun her capacity to express herself: a particularly striking development, given Elizabeth's usual repartee. [*AO1 for advancing the argument with a judiciously selected quote; AO2 for the close analysis of the language*].

- However, Elizabeth is not the only one overrun by the emotions love induces: Mr Darcy is also plunged into a state of emotional intensity. He is described here 'as a man violently in love' – the word 'violently' suggesting that the love has almost careered out of control – and, after learning that Elizabeth reciprocates his feelings, his response seems to transcend language: we are told of a 'heartfelt delight [that] diffused over his face.' Indeed, the observation that 'there was too much to be thought, and felt, and said, for attention to any other objects,' with its powerful use of breathless polysyndeton, perfectly captures how love has left both individuals bowled over with emotions.[2] Austen seems to differentiate stylistically between a proposal without love, such as Mr Collins' to Elizabeth or Mr Elton's to Emma in Austen's eponymous novel, and a serious and loving proposal such as Mr Darcy's to Elizabeth in this extract or Bingley's to Jane, by writing the former proposals through dialogue between the couple, and the latter by only third-person narrative, to show that the happiness felt by Austen's loving couples is too overwhelming to put into words. [*AO1 for advancing the argument with a judiciously selected quote; AO2 for the close analysis of the language and for discussing how form and structure shapes meaning*].

- Elsewhere in the novel: In many respects, the emotional response seen here is Austen's method of communicating the sincerity of the pair's love. It is perhaps unsurprising that in the novel's final chapter, the reader is informed that '[Mr Wickham's] affection [to his wife, Lydia] soon sunk into indifference.' Whereas the love Elizabeth and Mr Darcy, share inspires overwhelming emotion, Mr Wickham's feelings toward Lydia quickly become those of boredom and neglect: possible evidence that his purported love for Lydia had never been genuine. [*AO1 for advancing the argument with a judiciously selected quote*].

Theme/Paragraph Three: Austen presents love as a phenomenon capable not only of overcoming social and class divisions, but also opposition by influential family members, whilst having a mellowing effect on those it touches.

- Austen highlights in this passage how the attempts by the status-obsessed Lady Catherine de Bourgh to frustrate any romance between Mr Darcy and the lower-status Elizabeth Bennet in fact ironically precipitate their union. Mr Darcy mentions how Lady Catherine had told him about 'her journey to

Longbourn' to try and get Elizabeth to reveal whether Mr Darcy had proposed to her. During that meeting, two chapters earlier in the novel, Lady Catherine lectures Elizabeth on how her daughter and Mr Darcy are destined to be together, and dismisses Elizabeth as a 'young woman without family, connections, or fortune.' Indeed, Lady Catherine's disdain for Elizabeth is reiterated in this passage, too: that she dwelled 'emphatically on [Elizabeth's] every expression' seems to indicate an obsessive distaste for the individual under her scrutiny. [*AO1 for advancing the argument with a judiciously selected quote; AO2 for the close analysis of the language*].

- Austen, through this ironic manoeuvring, lampoons Lady Catherine's belief that love ought to abide by class divides. Yet, more importantly, Austen also explores how love actively transcends these barriers. Whereas Mr Darcy had previously dwelt on the idea that Elizabeth and her family were beneath him – during his first proposal to Elizabeth, he asks 'could you expect me to rejoice in the inferiority of your connections?' – as his love matures, he realises the folly of his prideful stance, and comes to value Elizabeth's social standing: 'I respect them,' he explicitly says of her family here. The reader might surmise that through helping Lydia for Elizabeth's sake, Mr Darcy has come to know and understand her family better; so, arguably, love has softened him, and it is presented here as a force for change and personal improvement. [*AO1 for advancing the argument with a judiciously selected quote; AO2 for the close analysis of the language*].

Conclusion

"Austen presents the main love narrative in *Pride and Prejudice* as one with a happy ending, although there are many challenges to be met by both Darcy and Elizabeth on their journey. Contrasted with their search for real, lasting love are other, venal examples of what lack of love can mean: the ill-matched Mr and Mrs Bennet, the Collins' marriage of convenience and the short-lived passion of the Wickhams. Austen, through these unhappy examples, is arguably showing how real happiness can only be found in couples who have a mutual loving respect for each other."

'" Now, be sincere; did you admire me for my impertinence?"'

Another illustration from C. E. Brock. It
depicts a scene in Chapter Sixty that sees
Elizabeth playfully tease Mr Darcy.

NOTES

ESSAY PLAN ONE

1. Foibles refers to flaws and/or eccentricities.
2. If someone is mercurial, it means they are changeable and volatile of opinion or mood.
3. Hyperbole is another word for exaggeration.
4. To transgress means to exceed a limit or to break a rule.

ESSAY PLAN TWO

1. We would call Marry Wollstonecraft a proto-feminist because she was living before feminism existed as a formal body of thought, yet her work anticipates a number of feminist values and ideas.
2. A patriarchy is a society ruled and dominated by men. As a result, the phrase "patriarchal expectations" refers to the codes of behaviour a male dominated society expect those living within it to adhere to.
3. To be pedantic is to be obsessively worried about detailed.

ESSAY PLAN THREE

1. Niccolò Machiavelli was a Renaissance philosopher who wrote about intricacies of political scheming. Therefore, to be Machiavellian is to be someone adept at scheming and manipulating. However, I have referred to Mrs Bennet as a 'would-be Machiavellian schemer' because she is arguably not so effective at scheming as she might wish to be!
2. What is a "trochaic word"?

   You may have heard of the word "iamb" before, which refers to an unstressed syllable followed by a stressed syllable. The word be**cause** is an iambic word, since the stress (or the "ictus") is on the second syllable.

   A "trochee," on the other hand, is when the stress is on the first syllable, but not on the second syllable. Take the name **Aus**ten, for instance. It is a trochaic word, as the stress (or ictus) is on the first syllable.

ESSAY PLAN FOUR

1. An epiphany is something akin to a grand realisation. An epiphanic moment is a moment in which such a realisation takes place.

ESSAY PLAN FIVE

1. To be meticulous is to be intensely thorough and attentive to the details.
2. When I talk about the narrator's free and indirect style, I am referring to the way in which the narrator recounts events in the third person, and yet sometimes seems to be inside Elizabeth's head, almost as if she has direct access to Elizabeth's thoughts. We are not being given unmediated first-person access to Elizabeth's thoughts, but with the free indirect narrative we are being given the next best thing.
3. A surrogate is a bit like a substitute. A surrogate mother, for instance, is a mother who raises a child in the event the biological mother is not available to do so. In this instance, I am suggesting that Elizabeth arguably replaces us as the reader, as she sets about interpreting texts and events on our behalf.

ESSAY PLAN SIX

1. A cataclysm is a hugely disastrous event.
2. Salaciousness refers to thing to do with sexually inappropriate behaviour.
3. Staccato is a word that is chiefly used in music. However, when used to describe language, it implies the words or phrase are short and jarring.
4. To be exonerated is to be shown or proved not to be guilty.

ESSAY PLAN SEVEN

1. A paradigm is sort of like a model version of something. So a paradigmatic relationship would be the sort that other relationships might wish to emulate.
2. Polysyndeton is a Greek word and refers to a type of sentence constructions that makes use of a multitude of conjunctions (such as 'and,' 'but' and 'nor') to conjure an air of drama.

Printed in Great Britain
by Amazon

38276930R00047